Southern Living

prownies & bars

Pecan Pie Squares, page 12

Contents

Hello, Fellow Brownie Lovers!

We hope you enjoy your new brownie pan and the brownie and bar cookie recipes in this book. The pan is made of solid tin, which is known for even conduction of heat. The baking area of the pan measures 7½ inches square, and these recipes were developed especially for this pan. Follow these tips for brownie bliss:

- Line the bottom of your pan with parchment paper and spray the pan and paper with vegetable cooking spray for easier cleanup.
- Use butter or stick margarine when specified. Substituting reduced calorie, tub-style, or whipped margarine or butter will affect the texture and flavor.
- Use an oven thermometer to ensure that your oven is heating accurately; a few degrees make a difference.
- If you like soft chewy brownies, remove them from the oven at the lower end of the bake time. For firmer brownies, bake for the longer time suggested.
- Freeze brownies for several minutes before cutting to make them cut easier.
- Cut cooled brownies with a plastic knife for smoother edged brownies and to avoid scratching your pan. You'll never want to cut brownies with a regular knife again once you see the clean slices this humble plastic knife makes.
- Store brownies in an airtight container rather than a cookie jar, which hastens drying out. If you want to store them in the pan, wrap the pan airtightly.
- Wash the pan in hot soapy water after each use, and thoroughly dry it just after washing.
- Remember that bake times will change if you use a pan of a different size or made of a different material. Expect shorter brownies and shorter baking time in 8-inch square or larger pans.

Apple-Gingerbread Squares
Prep: 7 min., Cook: 40 min.

These tasty squares showcase all the best flavors of fall.

¼ cup butter, softened
⅓ cup granulated sugar
3 Tbsp. firmly packed dark brown sugar
1 large egg
1 cup all-purpose flour
1 tsp. crystallized ginger, minced
1 tsp. ground ginger
¾ tsp. baking soda
½ tsp. ground cinnamon
½ tsp. ground cloves
¼ tsp. salt
½ cup molasses
½ cup boiling apple cider
Ginger-Molasses Whipped Cream

1. Beat butter at medium speed with a handheld mixer until creamy; gradually add sugars, beating well. Add egg, beating until mixture is blended.

2. Add flour and next 8 ingredients; beat at medium speed until smooth. Pour into a greased and floured 7½-inch square pan.

3. Bake at 325° for 35 to 40 minutes or until a wooden pick inserted in center comes out clean. Cool on a wire rack. Cut into squares. Serve with Ginger-Molasses Whipped Cream. Makes 16 squares.

Ginger-Molasses Whipped Cream
Prep: 3 min.

½ cup whipping cream
1½ tsp. powdered sugar
1½ tsp. molasses
⅛ tsp. ground ginger

1. Beat all ingredients at high speed with a handheld mixer until soft peaks form. Makes 1 cup.

Lemon Squares
Prep: 7 min., Cook: 51 min.

1 cup all-purpose flour
¼ cup powdered sugar
½ cup butter
Dash of salt
1 cup granulated sugar
2 Tbsp. all-purpose flour
3 large eggs
1 Tbsp. grated lemon rind
3 Tbsp. fresh lemon juice
½ tsp. baking powder
Powdered sugar

1. Process first 4 ingredients in a food processor until dough forms a ball. Press dough into a greased 7½-inch square pan lined with parchment paper. Bake at 325° for 25 to 30 minutes or until golden.
2. Process granulated sugar and next 5 ingredients in a food processor until blended. Pour over crust. Bake at 325° for 21 minutes or until set. Cool completely; dust with additional powdered sugar, and cut into squares. Makes 16 squares.

Easy to transport, these
sunny-looking treats
are a perfect picnic snack.

Cranberry-Caramel Streusel Squares

Prep: 10 min., Cook: 48 min.

Take these out when the edges get dark; the center will set up as the pan cools off.

$1/2$	cup fresh or frozen cranberries
5	Tbsp. granulated sugar
1	cup all-purpose flour
$1/4$	tsp. baking soda
1	cup uncooked regular oats
$1/4$	cup firmly packed light brown sugar
$1/2$	cup butter or margarine, melted
$1/2$	cup chopped dates
$1/3$	cup chopped pecans
$2/3$	cup caramel topping
2	Tbsp. all-purpose flour

1. Stir together cranberries and 1 tablespoon sugar in a small bowl; set aside. Combine remaining 4 Tbsp. sugar, 1 cup flour, and next 3 ingredients; stir in melted butter until crumbly. Reserve $1/2$ cup flour mixture. Press remaining mixture into bottom of a lightly greased $7\frac{1}{2}$-inch square pan. Bake at 350° for 18 minutes or until lightly browned.

2. Sprinkle with dates, pecans, and reserved cranberry mixture. Stir together caramel topping and 2 tablespoons flour in a small bowl; spoon over top. Sprinkle with reserved flour mixture. Bake at 350° for 26 to 30 minutes or until lightly browned. Cool completely in pan on a wire rack. Cut into squares. Makes 16 squares.

These colorful squares make an eye-catching end to a holiday meal.

Raspberry Squares
Prep: 8 min., Cook: 30 min.

●○●○●○●○●●○●○●○●○○●○●●○

6   Tbsp. butter, softened
½   cup firmly packed light brown sugar
¾   cup all-purpose flour
¼   tsp. baking soda
¼   tsp. salt
¾   cup uncooked quick-cooking oats
½   cup seedless raspberry jam

1. Beat butter at medium speed with an electric mixer until creamy; gradually add sugar, beating well. Combine flour and next 3 ingredients; add to butter mixture, beating well.
2. Press two-thirds of crumb mixture into a 7½-inch square pan. Bake at 400° for 10 minutes. Remove from oven; spread raspberry jam over crust. Sprinkle with remaining one-third crumb mixture, and bake 20 more minutes. Let cool completely on a wire rack. Cut into squares. Makes 16 squares.

Strawberry Squares: Substitute ½ cup strawberry preserves for the raspberry preserves.

A crumbly oat mixture bakes into a
pebbly topping over raspberry preserves
on a shortbread crust.

Cherry-Walnut Snack Cake

Prep: 13 min., Cook: 20 min.

●●●●●●○●●○●●●●●●●○●○○●●●●●

"Cut in" is the term for mixing a cold fat, such as butter or short-ening, with dry ingredients until the mixture is crumbly. We use a pastry blender but you can use two forks.

½   cup dried cherries
1   cup all-purpose flour
½   cup brown sugar blend, firmly packed (we tested
      with Splenda)
6   Tbsp. butter, cut into cubes
½   cup sour cream
1   large egg, lightly beaten
½   tsp. baking soda
½   cup chopped walnuts

1. Pour boiling water to cover over dried cherries; let stand 10 minutes. Drain well, and set aside.

2. While cherries stand, combine flour and brown sugar blend in a large bowl; cut in butter with a pastry blender until crumbly. Press 1¼ cups crumb mixture into a lightly greased 7½-inch square pan.

3. Stir together sour cream, egg, and baking soda; add to remaining crumb mixture in bowl, stirring just until dry ingredients are moistened. Stir in drained cherries. Pour sour cream mixture over prepared crust in pan; sprinkle with walnuts.

4. Bake at 350° for 15 to 20 minutes or until a wooden pick inserted in center comes out clean. Let cool completely in pan on a wire rack, and cut into squares. Makes 9 servings.

Salted Peanut Chews
Prep: 13 min., Cook: 20 min.

●●◦●●◦●●●●●●◦●●◦●◦●●●●

²/₃ cup all-purpose flour
¼ tsp. baking powder
¼ tsp. baking soda
¼ tsp. salt
6 Tbsp. firmly packed brown sugar
¼ cup butter, softened
2 egg yolks
½ tsp. vanilla extract
1½ cups miniature marshmallows
1 cup peanut butter morsels
¼ cup light corn syrup
2 Tbsp. butter
1 tsp. vanilla extract
1 cup crisp rice cereal
1 cup salted roasted peanuts

1. Combine first 8 ingredients in a large mixing bowl. Beat at low speed with an electric mixer until crumbly. Press into an ungreased 7½-inch square pan. Bake at 350° for 12 to 14 minutes or until lightly browned. Sprinkle with marshmallows; bake 2 more minutes or until marshmallows begin to puff. Cool in pan on a wire rack.

2. Combine peanut butter morsels and next 3 ingredients in a large saucepan; cook over low heat, stirring constantly, until smooth. Remove from heat; stir in cereal and peanuts. Spread cereal mixture over marshmallows. Cool completely in pan on wire rack. Cut into bars. Makes 12 bars.

This salty-sweet combination will please everyone.

Crispy No-Bake Peanut Bars

Prep: 6 min., Cook: 2 min., Other: 1 hr.

●●●●◌●◌●●●●◌●◌●◌●●●●

It's easy to whip up a batch of these sweet and crunchy favorites.

- ½ cup sugar
- ½ cup light corn syrup
- ½ cup creamy peanut butter
- ½ tsp. vanilla extract
- 3½ cups crisp rice cereal squares
- ½ cup peanuts

1. Combine sugar, corn syrup, and peanut butter in a glass bowl; microwave at HIGH 2 minutes or until melted, stirring once. Stir in vanilla.

2. Fold in cereal and peanuts. Spread mixture into a lightly greased 7½-inch square pan. Cover and chill 1 hour or until set. Cut into bars. Makes 12 bars.

Pecan Pie Squares

Prep: 9 min., Cook: 43 min.

●●●●◌●◌●●●●◌●◌●◌●●●●

Honey adds a subtle flavor to traditional pecan pie ingredients in this decadent treat.

- 1 cup all-purpose flour
- ⅓ cup powdered sugar
- ½ cup butter, slightly softened
- ¼ cup firmly packed light brown sugar
- ¼ cup honey
- ⅓ cup butter
- 1 Tbsp. whipping cream
- 1¾ cups chopped pecans

1. Combine flour and powdered sugar in a medium bowl; cut in softened butter using a pastry blender or fork just until mixture resembles coarse meal. Pat mixture into a lightly greased 7½-inch square pan.

2. Bake at 350° for 18 to 20 minutes or until edges are lightly browned. Cool slightly.

3. Combine brown sugar and next 3 ingredients in a small saucepan; bring to a boil over medium-high heat. Stir in pecans; pour filling over prepared crust. Bake at 350° for 20 to 23 minutes or until golden and bubbly. Cool completely in pan on a wire rack. Cut into squares. Makes 16 squares.

Caramel Mud Pie Brownies

Prep: 11 min.; Cook: 44 min.; Other: 1 hr., 15 min.

●●◉◎◦●●◉●◉◎◦◉●◉◦●●◉●●

The combination of caramel and chocolate always creates a delectable flavor combination.

2   large eggs
³⁄₄   cup butter, melted and divided
1   cup granulated sugar
¹⁄₄   tsp. salt
¹⁄₂   tsp. vanilla extract
²⁄₃   cup all-purpose flour
¹⁄₄   cup plus 2 Tbsp. unsweetened cocoa, divided
24   caramels (we tested with Kraft)
¹⁄₄   cup plus 2 Tbsp. milk, divided
1¹⁄₂ cups chopped pecans, toasted
3   large marshmallows
¹⁄₂   cup powdered sugar

1. Whisk together eggs, ¹⁄₂ cup butter, and next 3 ingredients in a large bowl. Add flour and ¹⁄₄ cup cocoa, blending well. Spread into a greased 7¹⁄₂-inch square pan. Bake at 350° for 35 to 40 minutes or until a wooden pick inserted in center comes out clean. Cool on a wire rack.

2. Microwave caramels and ¹⁄₄ cup milk in a large glass bowl at HIGH 1 minute or until melted. Stir to combine. Stir in pecans, and spread evenly over brownies. Chill 15 minutes or until set.

3. Combine marshmallows and remaining ¹⁄₄ cup butter, 2 tablespoons cocoa, and 2 tablespoons milk in a medium saucepan. Cook over medium heat, stirring constantly until mixture is smooth and thoroughly heated. Remove from heat.

4. Beat marshmallow mixture and powdered sugar with an electric mixer until smooth. Spread evenly over caramel mixture. Chill 1 hour or until chocolate is completely set. Cut into squares. Makes 16 brownies.

Chewy Praline-Chocolate Fudge Bars

Prep: 20 min., Cook: 23 min.

●●○●●○●○●●●●●●○●○●●●●

½ cup butter, softened
½ cup firmly packed light brown sugar
½ tsp. vanilla extract
1 cup all-purpose flour
½ cup chopped pecans, toasted
Praline Fudge Icing
1 cup semisweet chocolate morsels, divided
2 Tbsp. milk

1. Stir butter until creamy; gradually add brown sugar and
vanilla, stirring until light and fluffy. Stir in flour and pecans.
Press dough into an ungreased 7½-inch square pan.
2. Bake at 350° for 17 minutes or until brown around the edges.
3. When brownies are done, sprinkle ⅔ cup chocolate morsels
over warm bars. Spoon warm Praline Fudge Icing over chocolate morsels, spreading to edges with a spatula. Cool completely.
4. Combine remaining ⅓ cup chocolate morsels and milk in a
small microwave-safe bowl. Microwave at HIGH 20 seconds;
stir until smooth and drizzle over frosting. Let stand until
smooth. Cut into bars. Makes 12 bars.

Praline Fudge Icing

Prep: 5 min., Cook: 3 min., Other: 5 min.

¼ cup butter
½ cup firmly packed light brown sugar
¼ cup milk
1⅓ cups powdered sugar
¼ tsp. vanilla extract
½ cup chopped pecans, toasted

1. Melt butter in a saucepan over medium heat. Add brown
sugar; bring to a boil, and cook, stirring constantly, 1½ minutes.
Remove from heat.
2. Slowly stir in milk. Return to heat; bring to a boil, stirring
until smooth. Remove from heat; let stand 5 minutes. Gradually
add powdered sugar and vanilla; beat at medium speed with a
handheld mixer until smooth. Stir in pecans. Makes 1¼ cups.

Holiday Candy Squares

Prep: 15 min., Cook: 33 min.

●●●●●●●●●●●●●●●●●●●

The red and green candies that dot this rich bar add a festive touch to this holiday dessert—that is, while it lasts!

1   cup uncooked quick-cooking oats
¾   cup all-purpose flour
½   cup chopped pecans
½   cup firmly packed light brown sugar
½   tsp. baking soda
¼   tsp. salt
½   cup butter, melted
¾   cup red and green candy-coated chocolate pieces, divided
¾   cup sweetened condensed milk

1. Combine first 6 ingredients, stirring well. Add butter, and stir until mixture is crumbly. Reserve ¾ cup crumb mixture; press remaining crumb mixture into a lightly greased 7½-inch square pan. Bake at 375° for 6 minutes. Set aside on a wire rack. Reduce oven temperature to 350°.

2. Place 6 Tbsp. chocolate pieces in a microwave-safe bowl; microwave at HIGH 1 minute or until softened, stirring after 30 seconds. Press chocolate pieces with the back of a spoon until mashed. (The candies will almost be melted with pieces of color coating still visible.) Stir in condensed milk. Spread mixture evenly over crust in pan, leaving a ½-inch border on all sides.

3. Combine reserved ¾ cup crumb mixture and remaining 6 Tbsp. chocolate pieces; sprinkle evenly over chocolate mixture, and press lightly.

4. Bake at 350° for 25 to 27 minutes or until golden. Cool in pan on a wire rack. Cut into squares. Makes 16 squares.

Candy Bar Brownies
Prep: 12 min., Cook: 41 min., Other: 2 hr.

●●━━●●●●●●●●●●━●●

2   large eggs, lightly beaten
$\frac{2}{3}$ cup sugar
6   Tbsp. butter, melted
1   tsp. vanilla extract
$\frac{2}{3}$ cup all-purpose flour
$\frac{1}{4}$ tsp. baking powder
$\frac{1}{4}$ tsp. salt
2   Tbsp. unsweetened cocoa
2   (2.07-oz.) chocolate-coated caramel-peanut nougat
      bars, coarsely chopped
2   (1.55-oz.) milk chocolate bars, finely chopped

1. Stir together first 4 ingredients in a medium bowl.
2. Combine flour and next 3 ingredients; stir into sugar mixture. Fold in chopped nougat bars. Spoon batter into a 7½-inch square pan lined with parchment paper; sprinkle chopped chocolate bars over batter.
3. Bake at 325° for 38 to 40 minutes or until brownies begin to pull away from sides of pan. Let cool completely in pan on a wire rack. Cut into squares. Makes 16 brownies.

A parchment paper-lined
pan ensures these
candy-packed
brownies can be
removed with ease.

Gooey Turtle Bars
Prep: 7 min., Cook: 25 min.

●●○●○●●●●●●●●○●●●

Quick and simple, this recipe minimizes fuss. Combine crust ingredients right in the pan; then sprinkle and drizzle toppings.

1   cup graham cracker crumbs
¼   cup butter, melted
1   cup semisweet chocolate morsels
½   cup pecan pieces
½   cup bottled caramel topping

1. Stir together crumbs and butter in an ungreased 7½-inch square pan, and press crumbs firmly in pan. Sprinkle evenly with chocolate morsels and pecans.
2. Microwave caramel topping at HIGH 30 seconds or until hot; stir well, and drizzle over pecans. Bake at 350° for 25 minutes; let cool in pan on a wire rack. Chill at least 30 minutes; cut into squares. Makes 16 bars.

No bowls needed—
cleanup is easy with this recipe!

Mint Julep Brownies
Prep: 10 min., Cook: 44 min., Other: 5 min.

¾   cup butter
3   (1-oz.) unsweetened chocolate baking squares
3   large eggs
1½ cups sugar
1   cup all-purpose flour
½   tsp. salt
2   Tbsp. bourbon
¾   tsp. peppermint extract
1   Tbsp. powdered sugar

1. Melt butter and chocolate in a medium saucepan over low heat, stirring until smooth. Let cool 5 minutes.
2. Whisk together eggs and sugar in a medium bowl. Add chocolate mixture, flour, and next 3 ingredients; whisk well. Pour batter into a greased 7½-inch square pan. Bake at 325° for 44 minutes. (Brownies are fudgy; wooden pick inserted in center will not come out clean.) Cool completely in pan on a wire rack. Cut into squares, and sprinkle with powdered sugar. Makes 16 brownies.

The texture of these oh-so-rich squares is more like fudge than a traditional brownie.

Amaretto-Walnut Brownies

Prep: 9 min., Cook: 45 min.

●●●■●●■●●●●●●●●●●●●●●

The almond liqueur gives these tasty brownies a distinctive flavor surprise.

½ cup chopped walnuts
½ cup butter
2 (1-oz.) unsweetened chocolate baking squares, coarsely chopped
1 cup sugar
⅛ tsp. salt
3 large eggs
1½ tsp. vanilla extract
¼ cup almond liqueur (we tested with Amaretto)
1 cup all-purpose flour

1. Place walnuts on a 15- x 10-inch jelly-roll pan. Bake at 350° for 6 minutes or until toasted.
2. Melt butter and chocolate in a heavy 2-quart saucepan over medium heat. Stir in sugar and salt until blended; remove pan from heat. Add eggs, vanilla, and liqueur; stir together until blended. Stir in walnuts and flour. Pour into a lightly greased 7½-inch square pan.
3. Bake at 325° for 45 minutes or until brownie pulls away from sides of the pan. Cool completely on a wire rack. Cut into squares. Makes 16 brownies.

Chocolate-Cream Cheese Swirl Brownies
Prep: 24 min., Cook: 45 min.

●●━●●━●━●━●●●━●●●━●━●●━●●

*It's a good idea to test these brownies in several places.
If your wooden pick touches a chocolate chip, the pick
won't come out clean.*

2   (1-oz.) unsweetened chocolate baking squares,
    chopped
2   (1-oz.) semisweet chocolate baking squares,
    chopped
2   Tbsp. butter
1   (3-oz.) package cream cheese, softened
2   Tbsp. butter, softened
¾   cup sugar, divided
1   Tbsp. all-purpose flour
3   large eggs
½   tsp. vanilla extract
⅔   cup semisweet chocolate morsels, divided
1   tsp. vanilla extract
¼   cup all-purpose flour
¼   tsp. baking powder
¼   tsp. salt

1. Combine first 3 ingredients in a small microwave-safe bowl;
cover with a small piece of wax paper. Microwave at LOW 30
seconds; stir until smooth, and set aside.
2. Whisk together cream cheese and 2 Tbsp. butter until
creamy; gradually whisk in 6 Tbsp. sugar and 1 Tbsp. flour until
smooth. Whisk in 1 egg and ½ tsp. vanilla until smooth. Whisk
in ⅓ cup chocolate morsels; set cream cheese batter aside.
3. Place remaining 6 Tbsp. sugar in a medium bowl. Whisk in
warm chocolate mixture until smooth. Whisk in remaining 2
eggs and 1 tsp. vanilla. In a separate bowl, whisk together ¼ cup
flour, baking powder, and salt; add to chocolate mixture, whisking until smooth. Stir in remaining ⅓ cup chocolate morsels.
4. Spoon chocolate batter in about 5 large portions into a lightly
greased 7½-inch square pan. Pour cream cheese batter over
chocolate batter. Swirl slightly with a small spatula. Bake at 325°
for 45 minutes or until a wooden pick comes out clean. Cool
completely on a wire rack. Cut into squares. Makes 12 brownies.

Chocolate Toffee Squares

Prep: 10 min., Cook: 47 min.

●━●━●━●━●━●━●━●━●━●━●━●━●━●━●

$1/4$ cup butter, melted
$1 1/3$ cups crushed teddy bear-shaped chocolate graham cracker cookies
3 (1.4-oz.) English toffee candy bars, crushed
$1/2$ cup semisweet chocolate morsels
$1/2$ cup chopped pecans
$1/4$ cup chopped walnuts
1 cup sweetened condensed milk

1. Line a $7 1/2$-inch square pan with heavy duty aluminum foil, allowing foil to extend over pan. Coat foil with cooking spray. Pour butter into pan. Sprinkle chocolate crumbs in pan; press firmly, and bake at 325° for 8 minutes.
2. Layer crushed candy bars and next 3 ingredients over crust in pan. Press layers down firmly. Pour condensed milk over nuts.
3. Bake at 325° for 36 to 39 minutes or until lightly browned. Cool completely in pan on a wire rack. Lift foil out of pan. Cut into squares. Makes 16 squares.

Lining with foil is an easy way to get these **ooey-gooey bars out of the pan** and makes cleanup a cinch.

Cappuccino Brownies
Prep: 5 min., Cook: 25 min.

●●●●●●●●●●●●●●●●●●●●

These delicious little treats received our highest rating.

2   (1-ounce) unsweetened chocolate baking squares
6   Tbsp. butter
1   cup sugar
2   large eggs
½   cup all-purpose flour
½   teaspoon vanilla extract
½   cup semisweet chocolate morsels
Cappuccino Buttercream Frosting
Garnish: chocolate shavings

1. Microwave chocolate squares and butter in a large microwave-safe bowl at HIGH 1 minute or until melted. Stir until smooth. Stir in sugar. Add eggs, whisking until blended.
2. Whisk in flour and vanilla; stir in chocolate morsels. Pour mixture into a lightly greased 7½-inch square pan.
3. Bake at 350° for 25 minutes or until a wooden pick inserted in center comes out almost clean. Cool completely on a wire rack.
4. Spread Cappuccino Buttercream Frosting evenly over top of cooled brownies. Garnish, if desired. Cut into 16 squares. Cover and chill, if desired. Makes 16 brownies.

Cappuccino Buttercream Frosting
Prep: 10 min.

2   (0.82-ounce) envelopes instant mocha cappuccino
    mix
3   tablespoons warm milk
¼   cup butter, softened
2⅔ cups powdered sugar

1. Dissolve cappuccino mix in warm milk in a small bowl, stirring to combine; cool completely. Pour milk mixture into a mixing bowl; add butter, whisking until well blended.
2. Gradually add powdered sugar, whisking until smooth and fluffy. Makes 1¼ cups.

Chocolate-Glazed Brownies
Prep: 7 min., Cook: 29 min., Other: 20 min.

●●●●●●●●●●●●●●●●●●●●

½ cup sugar
⅓ cup butter
2 Tbsp. water
1½ cups semisweet chocolate morsels, divided
½ tsp. vanilla extract
¾ cup all-purpose flour
¼ tsp. baking soda
¼ tsp. salt
1 large egg
½ cup chopped pecans, toasted

1. Cook first 3 ingredients in a medium saucepan over medium-high heat 2 minutes, stirring constantly with a whisk, or until sugar melts. Add 1 cup chocolate morsels and vanilla, stirring until mixture is smooth. Let cool 15 minutes.
2. Add flour, baking soda, and salt to cooled chocolate mixture, stirring until blended; stir in egg and pecans until blended. Spread batter into a lightly greased 7½-inch square pan.
3. Bake at 325° for 27 minutes. Sprinkle remaining ½ cup chocolate morsels evenly over warm brownies, and let stand 5 minutes to soften. Spread over top. Cool on a wire rack. Cut into squares. Makes 9 brownies.

These super-moist and chocolaty brownies boast chocolate morsels in both the batter and glaze.

Dark Chocolate Brownies

Prep: 11 min., Cook: 30 min.

●●●●●●●●●●●●●●●●●●●●●●

*Butter, walnuts, and chocolate morsels enrich these
delectable brownies.*

½ cup butter
3 oz. bittersweet chocolate (we tested with Nestlé
Chocolatier)
1 cup sugar
2 large eggs
1½ tsp. vanilla extract
½ cup all-purpose flour, divided
¾ cup chopped walnuts
½ cup semisweet chocolate morsels
⅛ tsp. salt

1. Microwave butter and bittersweet chocolate in a microwave-safe bowl at HIGH 1 minute or until chocolate melts, stirring mixture twice. Whisk in sugar, eggs, and vanilla.
2. Toss together 1½ teaspoons flour, walnuts, and chocolate morsels.
3. Stir remaining flour and salt into sugar mixture; add walnut mixture. Spread batter evenly into a lightly greased 7½-inch square pan.
4. Bake at 350° for 27 to 30 minutes. Cool on a wire rack, and cut into squares. Makes 12 brownies.

Chocolate Chip Cheesecake Bars

Prep: 6 min., Cook: 35 min., Other: 4 hr.

Watch the crust carefully to make sure it doesn't overbake.

½ cup all-purpose flour
3 Tbsp. light brown sugar
2 Tbsp. butter, softened
1 (8-oz.) package cream cheese, softened
1 (3-oz.) package cream cheese, softened
6 Tbsp. granulated sugar
1 large egg
3 Tbsp. sour cream
¼ tsp. vanilla extract
1 cup semisweet chocolate mini-morsels, divided

1. Whisk first 3 ingredients until well blended and crumbly. Pat mixture into a lightly greased 7½-inch square pan.

2. Bake at 350° for 11 minutes or until lightly browned.

3. Beat cream cheeses at medium speed with a handheld mixer until creamy. Gradually add granulated sugar, beating until well blended. Add egg, beating just until blended. Add sour cream, vanilla, and ½ cup chocolate morsels, beating just until blended. Pour over baked crust.

4. Bake at 350° for 21 to 23 minutes or until set. Let cool completely on a wire rack.

5. Microwave remaining chocolate morsels in a 2-cup glass measuring cup at HIGH 1 minute, stirring after 30 seconds. Stir until smooth. Cool slightly. Drizzle over cheesecake. Cover and chill at least 4 hours; cut into bars. Makes 15 bars.

Caramel-Coconut-Pecan Cheesecake Squares

Prep: 11 min., Cook: 38 min., Other: 8 hr.

●●●●●●●●●●●●●●●●●●●●●

1   cup graham cracker crumbs
¼   cup butter, melted
2   (8-oz.) packages cream cheese, softened
⅓   cup sugar
2   Tbsp. all-purpose flour
1   large egg
1½ tsp. vanilla extract
Quick Coconut-Pecan Frosting

1. Stir together graham cracker crumbs and butter; press into a lightly greased 7½-inch square pan. Bake at 350° for 8 minutes. Remove from oven.
2. Beat cream cheese at medium speed with an electric mixer until smooth. Combine sugar and flour; gradually add to cream cheese, beating just until blended. Add egg, beating until blended. Stir in vanilla. Pour mixture over prepared crust, spreading evenly to edges of pan.
3. Bake at 350° for 30 minutes or until set. Remove from oven, and cool on a wire rack. Pour warm Quick Coconut-Pecan Frosting over cheesecake, spreading evenly to edges of pan. Cover and chill 8 hours. Cut into squares. Makes 16 squares.

Quick Coconut-Pecan Frosting

Prep: 4 min., Cook: 15 min.

1   (14-oz.) can sweetened condensed milk
¼   cup firmly packed light brown sugar
¼   cup butter
½   tsp. vanilla extract
¾   cup sweetened flaked coconut
¾   cup chopped pecans, toasted

1. Place first 4 ingredients in a medium saucepan; bring to a boil, stirring constantly, over medium-low heat. Cook, stirring constantly, 10 minutes or until mixture reaches a puddinglike thickness. Remove from heat; stir in coconut and pecans. Makes 2 cups.

Toffee Cheesecake Bars
Prep: 14 min, Cook: 25 min., Other: 8 hr.

● ● ● ● ● ● ● ● ● ● ● ● ● ● ● ● ● ●

These bars are big enough and rich enough to serve with a knife and fork. For an easier pick-up treat, cut them into smaller portions.

$1/3$ cup butter, softened
$1/2$ cup firmly packed light brown sugar
1 cup all-purpose flour
$1/4$ cup chopped pecans
1 (8-oz.) package cream cheese, softened
$1/2$ cup granulated sugar
1 egg yolk
$1/2$ tsp. lemon juice
1 tsp. vanilla extract
$1/2$ cup crushed hard toffee candies (21 candies; we tested with Werther's)

1. Stir together butter and brown sugar until blended. Add flour, stirring well; stir in pecans. Set aside $1/2$ cup flour mixture. Press remaining flour mixture into a greased $7\frac{1}{2}$-inch square pan. Bake at 350° for 8 minutes or until lightly browned. Remove from oven, and set aside.

2. Beat cream cheese and next 4 ingredients at medium speed with an electric mixer until smooth. Spoon over prepared crust. Sprinkle reserved flour mixture evenly over batter. Bake at 350° for 15 to 17 minutes or until lightly browned and set; sprinkle immediately with crushed candies. Cool to room temperature in pan on a wire rack. Cover and chill 8 hours. Cut into bars. Makes 12 bars.

Note: Find Werther's candies on the candy aisle at a local drug store or grocery store. While filling bakes, crush candies in a large zip-top plastic freezer bag, using a meat mallet or rolling pin.

Double-Chocolate Brownies

Prep: 4 min., Cook: 30 min.

●●○●○●●●●●●○●○●●●●●

*Why use one kind of chocolate when two make
these brownies doubly delicious?*

½ cup butter, softened
1 cup sugar
2 large eggs
½ cup unsweetened cocoa
½ tsp. vanilla extract
½ cup all-purpose flour
½ cup chopped pecans
⅓ cup white chocolate morsels or semisweet
   chocolate morsels

1. Whisk butter until creamy; gradually add sugar, whisking
well. Add eggs, 1 at a time, beating just until blended.
2. Add cocoa and vanilla; whisk until blended. Gradually add
flour, whisking well.
3. Stir in pecans and chocolate morsels. Pour batter into a
greased 7½-inch square pan.
4. Bake at 325° for 28 to 30 minutes or until brownies start to
pull away from sides of pan. Cool and cut into squares. Makes
16 squares.

These chunky
delights will please
any chocolate lover.

Congo Squares
Prep: 13 min., Cook: 40 min.

●●━━○●●━●●●○●●○●━●●●━●●

We're not sure how this dessert got its name, but you'll love how it's loaded with chunky chocolate and cashews.

¼ cup butter, melted
1 cup firmly packed light brown sugar
2 large eggs, lightly beaten
½ tsp. vanilla extract
⅔ cup all-purpose flour
⅔ cup chocolate graham cracker crumbs
1 tsp. baking powder
½ cup salted cashews, chopped
1 cup semisweet chocolate chunks

1. Stir together first 4 ingredients in a medium bowl. Combine flour, graham cracker crumbs, and baking powder; add to butter mixture, stirring well. Stir in cashews and chocolate chunks (batter will be thick).
2. Spoon batter into a lightly greased 7½-inch square pan. Bake at 325° for 35 to 40 minutes or until set. Cool completely in pan on a wire rack. Cut into squares, using a sharp knife. Makes 16 squares.

Chocolate-Orange Cream Squares
Prep: 10 min., Cook: 18 min.

●●━━○●━●●●━●●○●●○●━●●●

½ cup butter or margarine
1 cup sugar
½ cup unsweetened cocoa
2 large eggs
1 tsp. orange liqueur or ¼ tsp. orange extract
½ cup all-purpose flour
2 (1-oz.) unsweetened chocolate baking squares, coarsely chopped
2 Tbsp. butter or margarine
Orange Cream Frosting

1. Melt ½ cup butter in a medium saucepan over low heat; remove from heat. Whisk together sugar and cocoa; whisk into melted butter until smooth. Whisk in eggs and liqueur until smooth; stir in flour. Pour batter into a greased 7½-inch square pan.

2. Bake at 350° for 16 to 18 minutes or until a wooden pick inserted in center comes out clean. Cool in pan on a wire rack.

3. Place chocolate and 2 Tbsp. butter in a small microwave-safe bowl. Microwave at HIGH 1 minute, stirring until smooth. Set aside to cool to spreading consistency.

4. Spread Orange Cream Frosting over uncut brownies. Drizzle cooled chocolate mixture over frosting. Dip a small spatula in hot water, and wipe dry. Using warm spatula, spread chocolate mixture thinly to cover frosting completely. Let stand until chocolate is set. Cut into squares. Store in refrigerator. Makes 16 squares.

Orange Cream Frosting
Prep: 5 min.

2 Tbsp. butter or margarine, softened
1½ cups sifted powdered sugar
½ tsp. grated orange rind
4 tsp. fresh orange juice

1. Whisk butter until creamy; gradually add powdered sugar, whisking well. Add rind and juice; whisk until blended. Makes ½ cup.

We spiked these brownies with orange liqueur, but you can use orange extract.

Amaretto-Walnut Brownies, page 21

Gooey Turtle Bars, pa

Chocolate-Cream Cheese
Swirl Brownies, page 22